Cole Porter Classics

By Frank Mantooth

TABLE OF CONTENTS

ISBN 0-7935-7530-3

HAL•LEONARD®
CORPORATION

7777 W. BLUEMOUND RD. P.O. BOX 13819 MILWAUKEE, WI 53213

T0050931

Visit Hal Leonard Online at
www.halleonard.com

INTRODUCTION

This play-along volume is a compilation of fifteen compositions by Cole Porter. These compositions are not tied to any single stylistic theme, e.g. "all blues" or "all bossas". Instead, this volume is a programmatic collection of jazz tunes representing various styles and written by Cole Porter.

This play-along offers the original melody along with the harmonic changes, a limited number of "blowing" choruses (sample choruses for improvisation), and a return to the melody (out-head). Usually a complete melody chorus is provided on both the front and end of the song.

Occasionally, the melody will D.S. back to the bridge rather than to the top of the form. This is a by-product of slower tempo tunes that by necessity of recording limitations needed to be approximately four minutes in length or less.

All tunes offer at least one complete sample chorus for improvisation. Please notice slight deviations between the written "out-head" and what is played on the enclosed recording. The musicians were requested to "personalize" the melodies as they might in a concert/club situation.

RECORDING INFORMATION

Natura Digital Recorders, Okmulgee, Oklahoma
David Smallwood and David Teegarden, Engineers

Musicians:
Kim Park, Saxophones
Lee Rucker, Trumpet and Flugelhorn
Kent Kidwell, Trombone
Danny Embrey, Guitar
Frank Mantooth, Piano
Bob Bowman, Bass
Tom Morgan, Drums

Scales/Modes for Improvisation
(from an F starting tone)

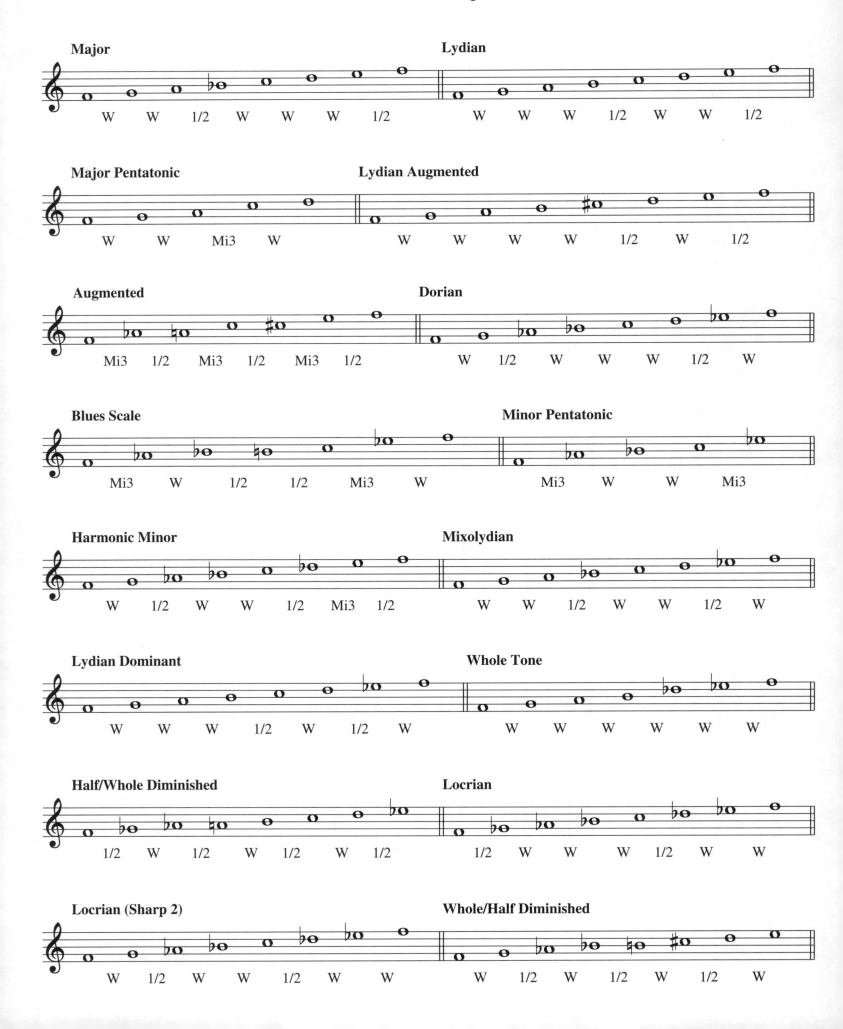

Some Scale or Mode Options for Improvisation:

Chord Symbol (major family)	Applicable Scale/Mode
Major Triads, Ma7, Ma9	Major Lydian Major Pentatonics
Ma6-9	Major Pentatonics
Ma7 or Ma9 with (#11) or ((♭5)	Lydian
Ma7 or Ma9 with (#5)	Lydian Augmented Augmented

Chord Symbol (minor family)	Applicable Scale/Mode
Minor Triads, Mi6, Mi7, Mi9, Mi11, and Mi13	Dorian Blues Scale Minor Pentatonics
Minor with (#7)	Harmonic Minor

Chord Symbol (dominant family)	Applicable Scale/Mode
7th, 9th, or13th	Mixolydian Major Pentatonics
with the alteration (#11) or (♭5)	Lydian Dominant
with the alterations (♭5) or (#5) or both	Whole Tone
with the alteration (♭9)	Half/Whole Diminished
with the alteration (#9)	Half/Whole Diminished Blues Scale Minor Pentatonics
Half Diminished Chords (Mi7(♭5))	Locrian Super Locrian (#2)
Diminished Chords	Whole/Half Diminished

I LOVE PARIS
from CAN-CAN

Words and Music by
COLE PORTER

Bb Instruments

7

Bb Instruments

ALL OF YOU
from SILK STOCKINGS

Words and Music by
COLE PORTER

Bb Instruments

Bb Instruments

WHAT IS THIS THING CALLED LOVE? ◆ 4

Words and Music by
COLE PORTER

B♭ Instruments

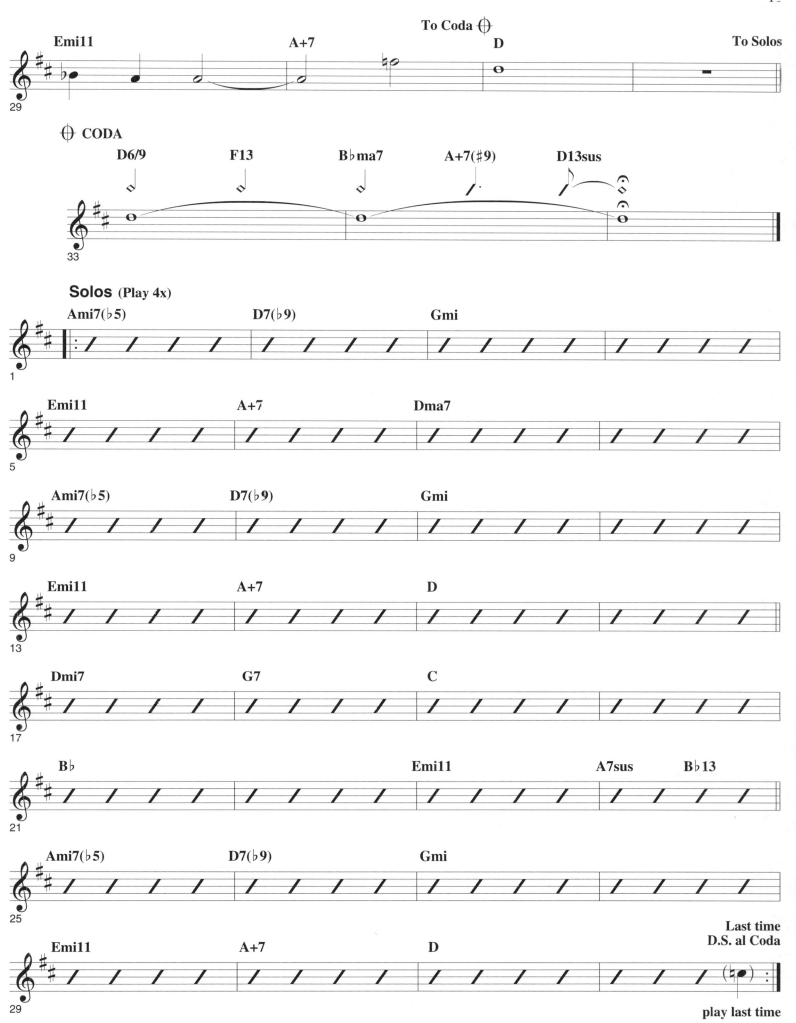

Bb Instruments

IT'S ALL RIGHT WITH ME ◆5

from CAN-CAN

Words and Music by
COLE PORTER

B♭ Instruments

B♭ Instruments

14

Bb Instruments

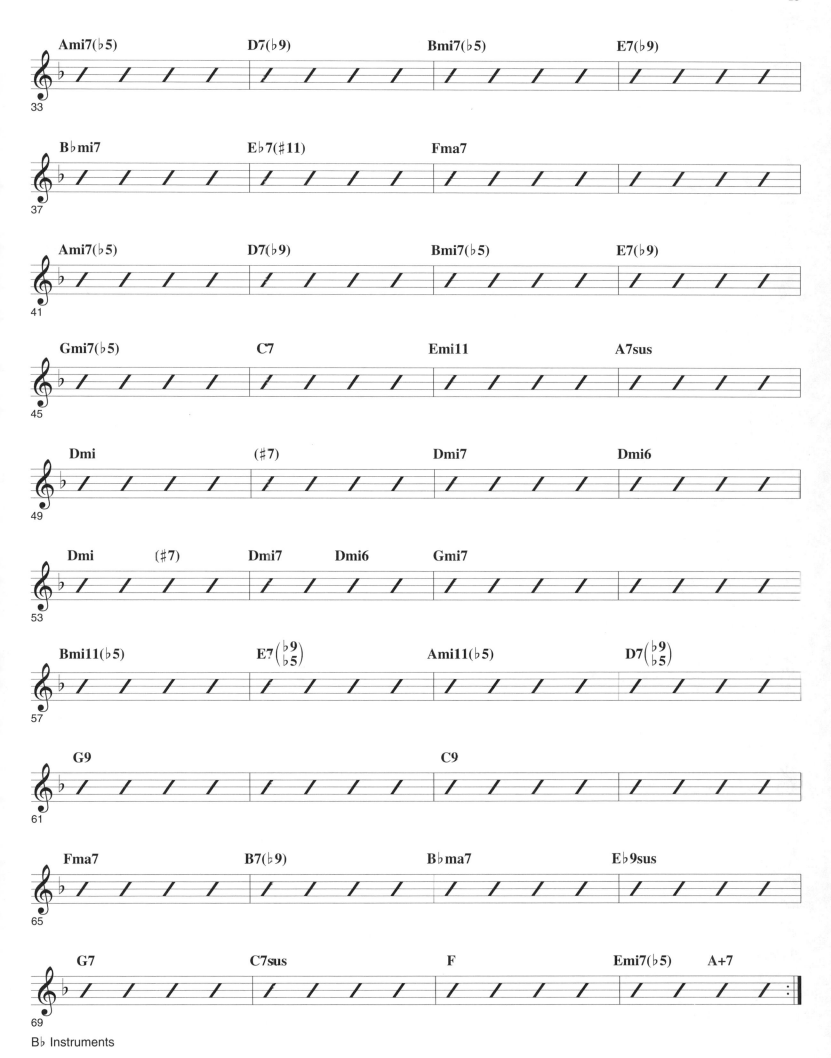

I CONCENTRATE ON YOU 6
from BROADWAY MELODY OF 1940

Words and Music by
COLE PORTER

Bb Instruments

Bb Instruments

18

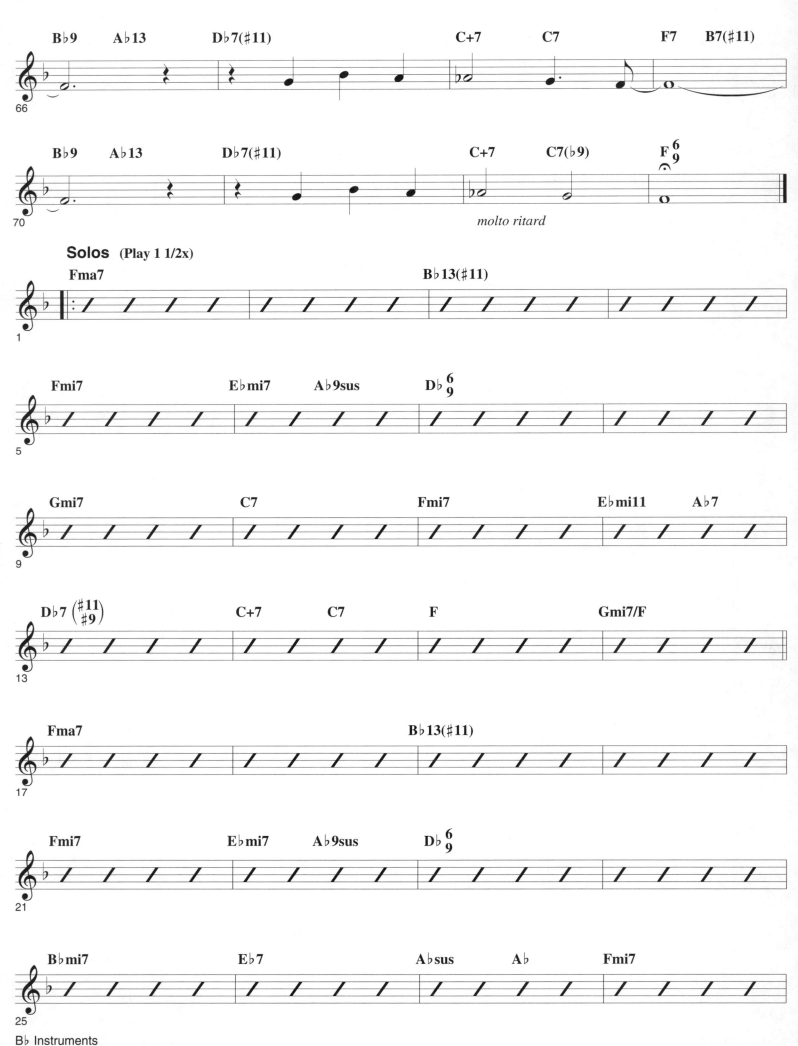

molto ritard

Solos (Play 1 1/2x)

B♭ Instruments

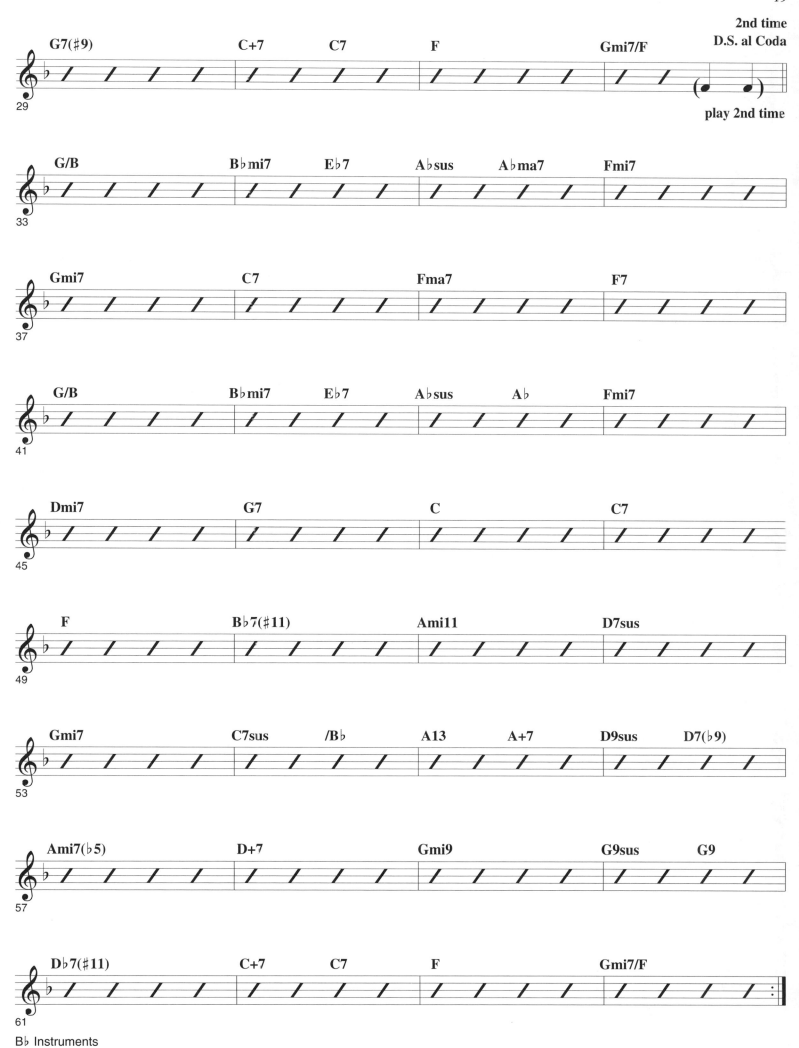

IT'S DE-LOVELY
from RED, HOT AND BLUE!

Words and Music by
COLE PORTER

Bb Instruments

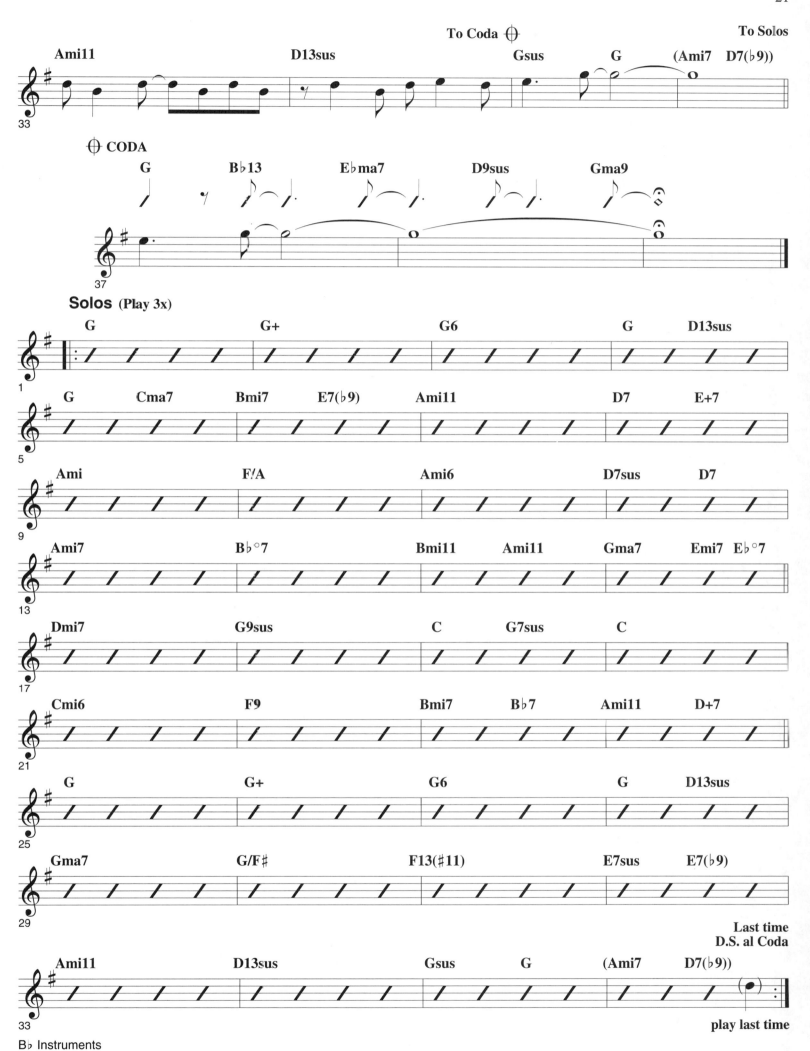

Bb Instruments

YOU'D BE SO NICE TO COME HOME TO ◆8

from SOMETHING TO SHOUT ABOUT

Words and Music by
COLE PORTER

Bb Instruments

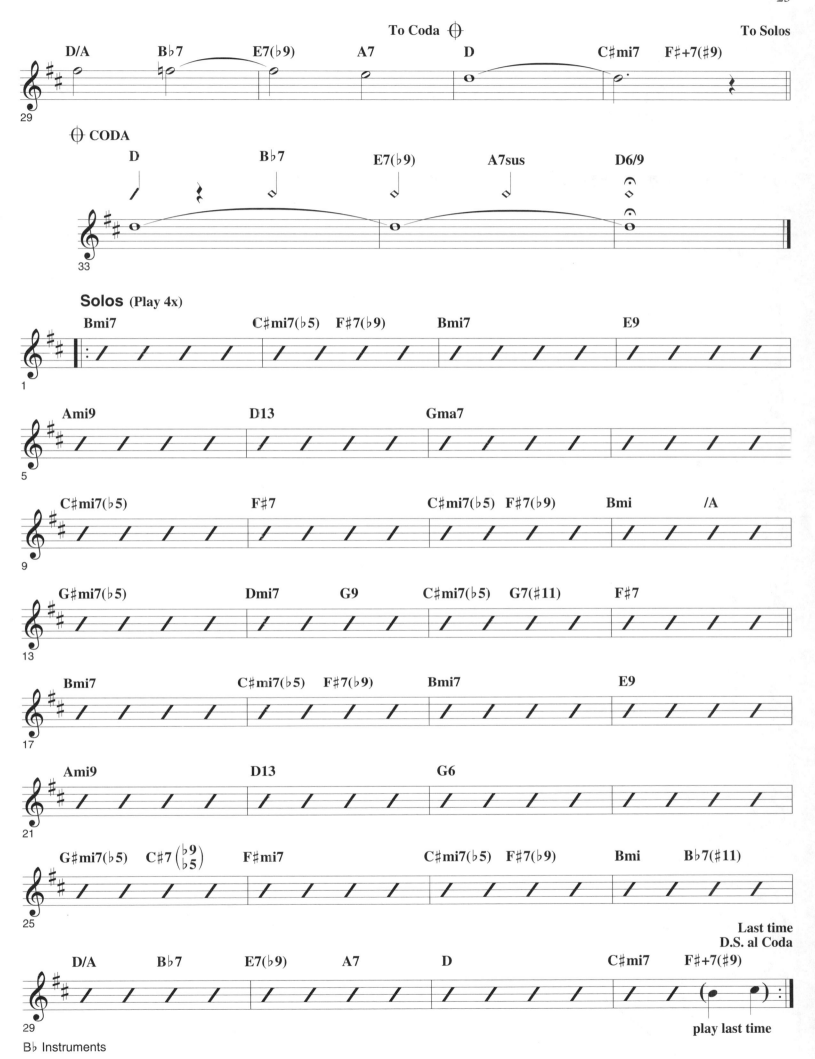

Bb Instruments

I LOVE YOU
from MEXICAN HAYRIDE

Words and Music by
COLE PORTER

Bb Instruments

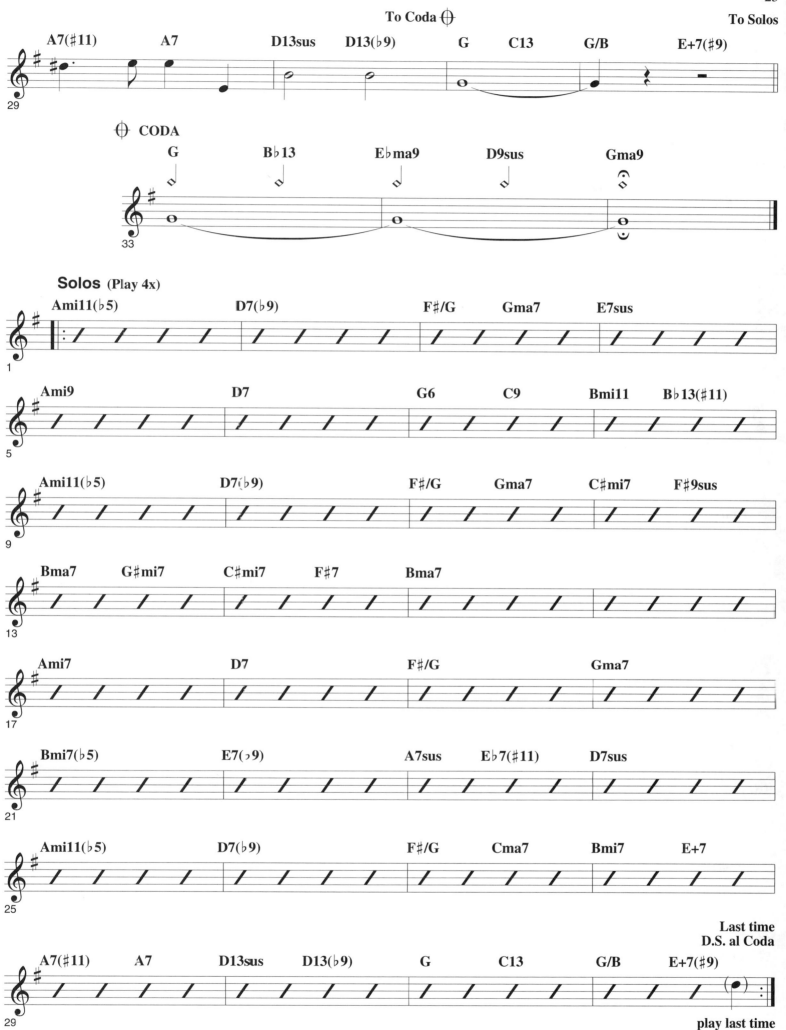

Bb Instruments

LOVE FOR SALE
from THE NEW YORKERS

Words and Music by
COLE PORTER

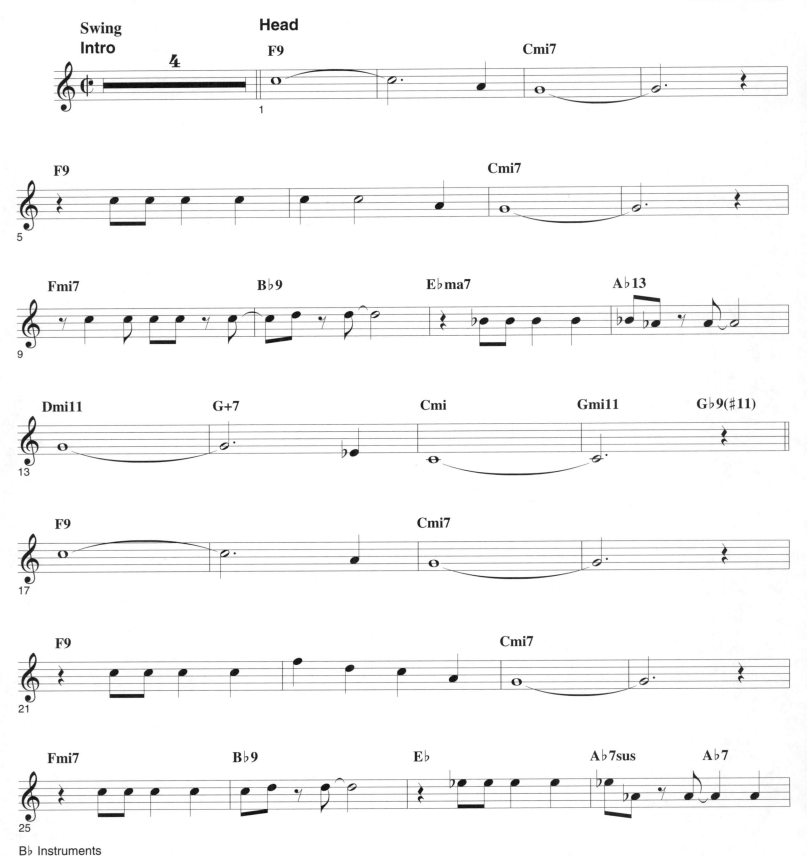

Bb Instruments

B♭ Instruments

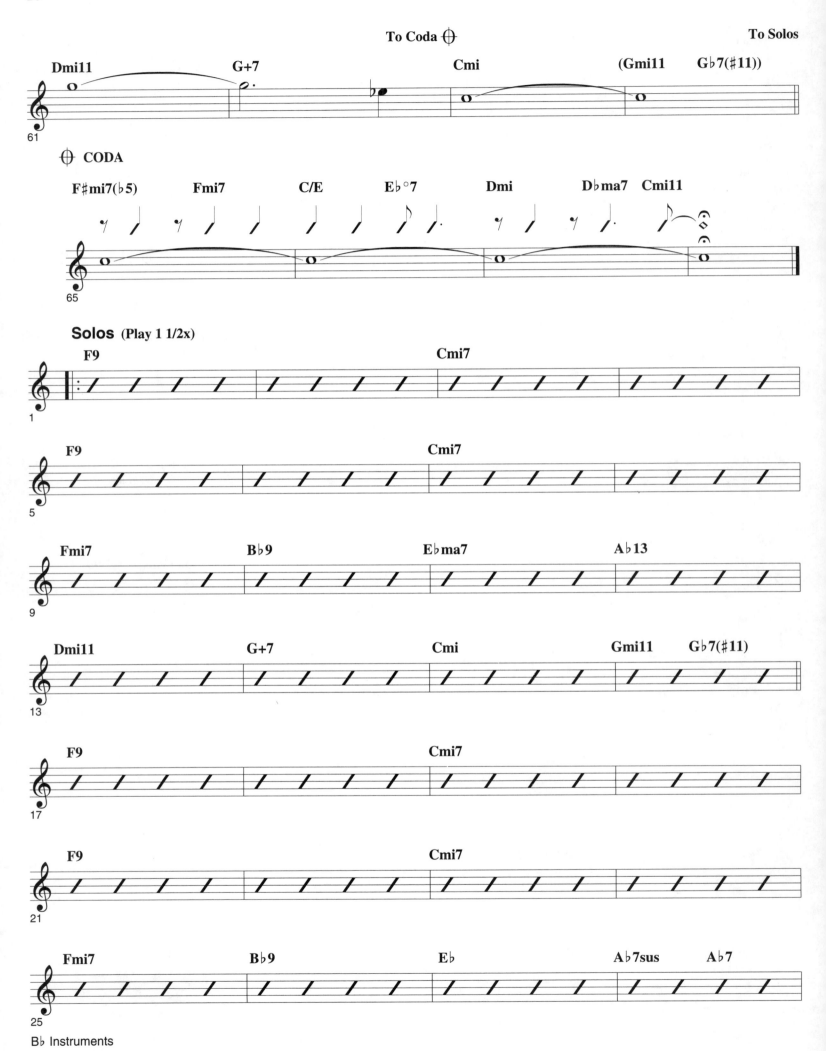

Bb Instruments

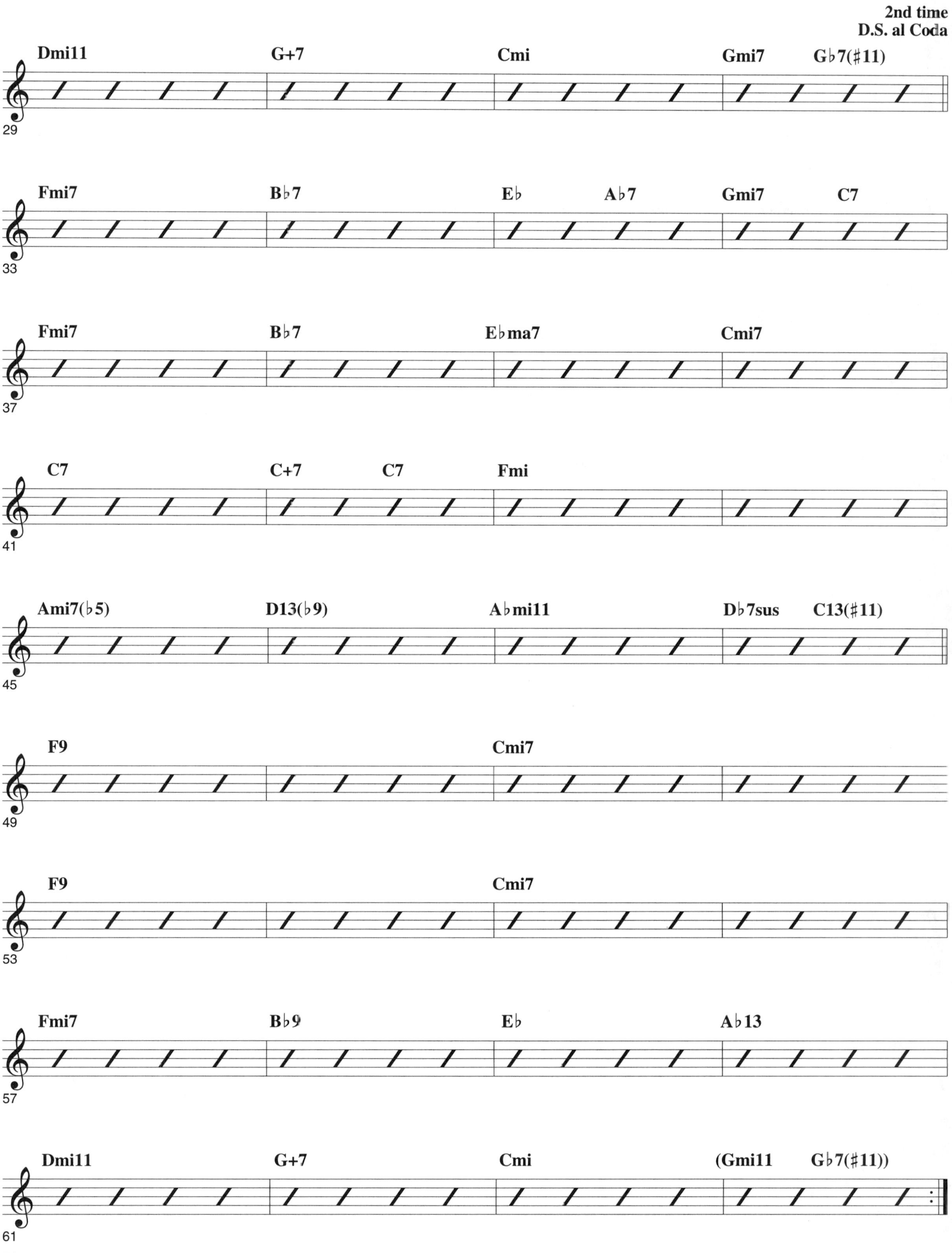

2nd time
D.S. al Coda

| Dmi11 | | G+7 | | Cmi | | Gmi7 | Gb7(#11) |

29

| Fmi7 | | Bb7 | | Eb | Ab7 | Gmi7 | C7 |

33

| Fmi7 | | Bb7 | | Ebma7 | | Cmi7 | |

37

| C7 | | C+7 | C7 | | Fmi | | |

41

| Ami7(b5) | | D13(b9) | | Abmi11 | | Db7sus | C13(#11) |

45

| F9 | | | | Cmi7 | | | |

49

| F9 | | | | Cmi7 | | | |

53

| Fmi7 | | Bb9 | | Eb | | Ab13 | |

57

| Dmi11 | | G+7 | | Cmi | | (Gmi11 | Gb7(#11)) |

61

Bb Instruments

SO IN LOVE

from KISS ME, KATE

Words and Music by
COLE PORTER

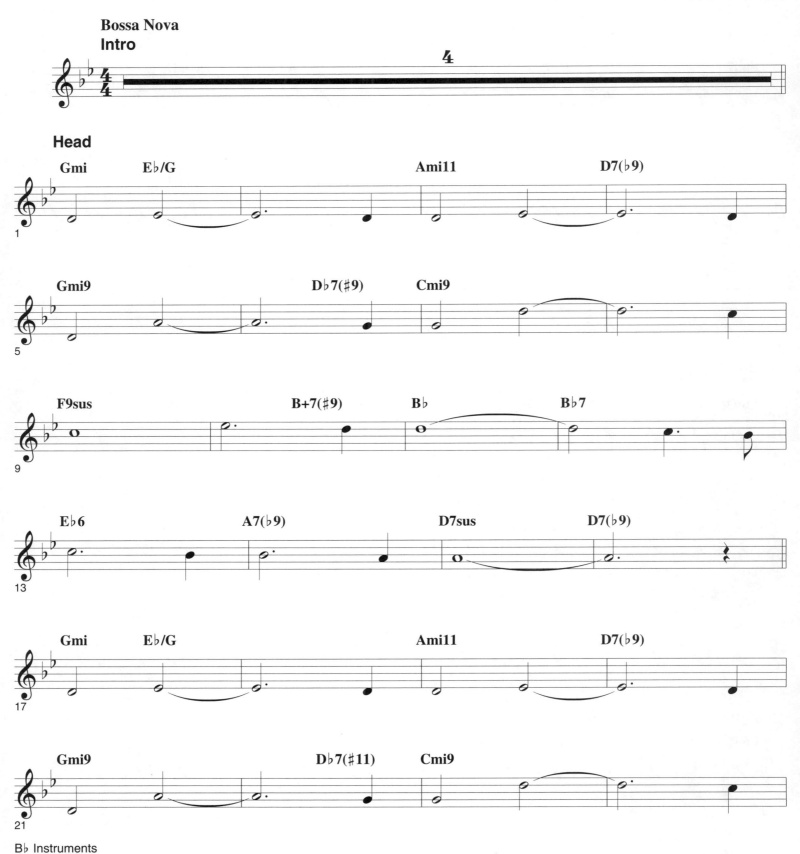

Bᵇ Instruments

31

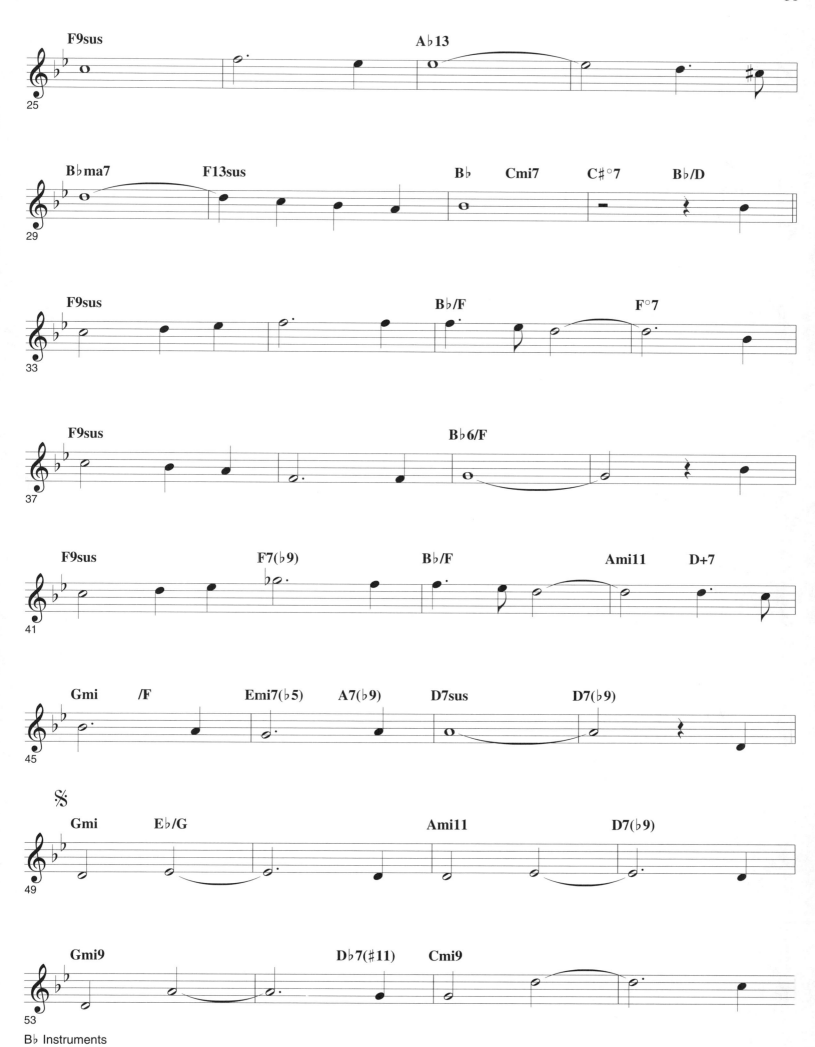

Bb Instruments

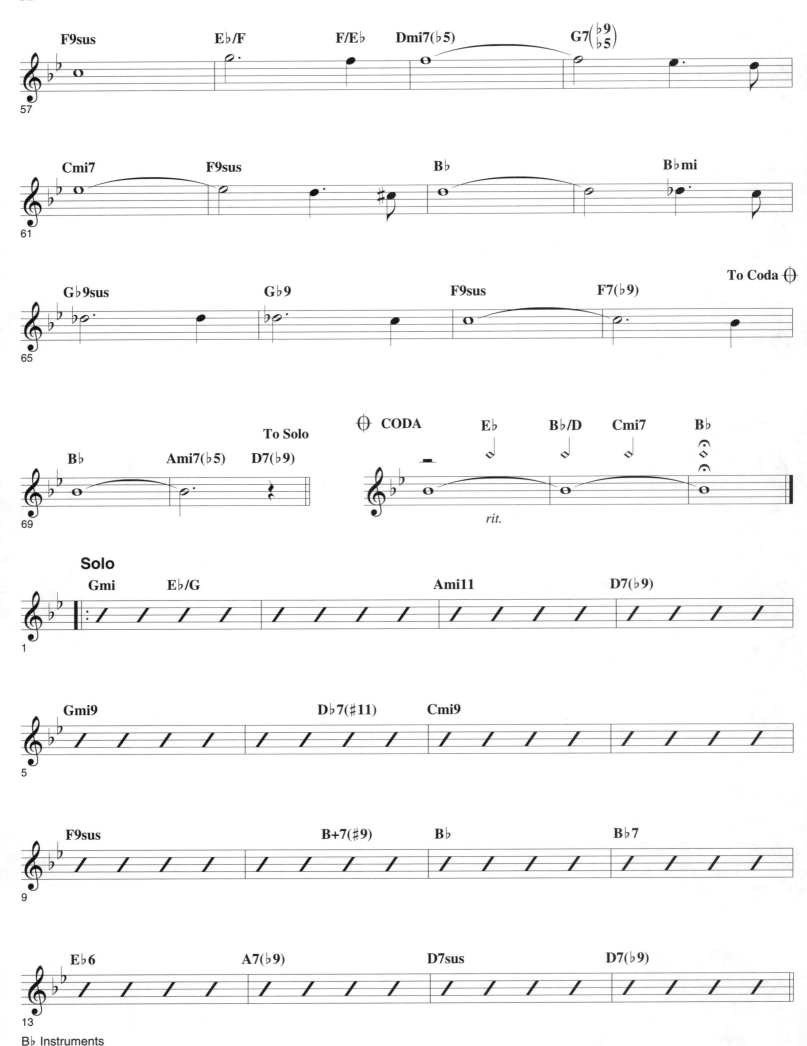

Bb Instruments

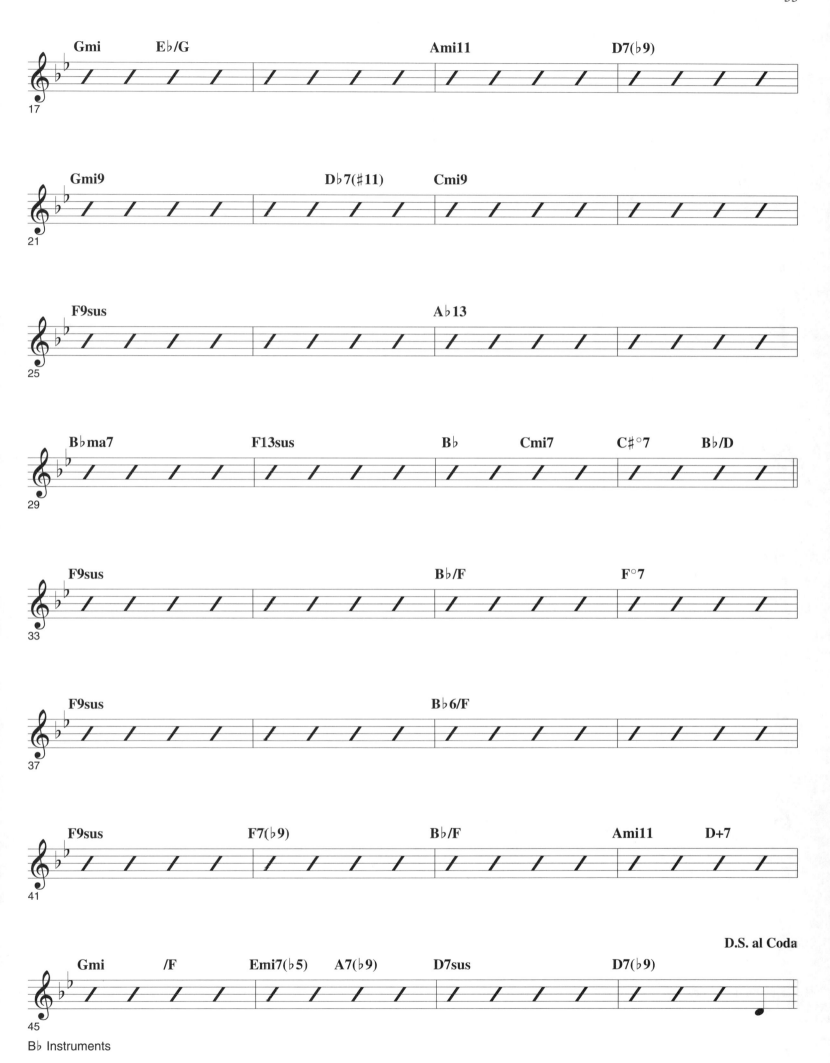

B♭ Instruments

I GET A KICK OUT OF YOU 12
from ANYTHING GOES

Words and Music by
COLE PORTER

Bb Instruments

Bb Instruments

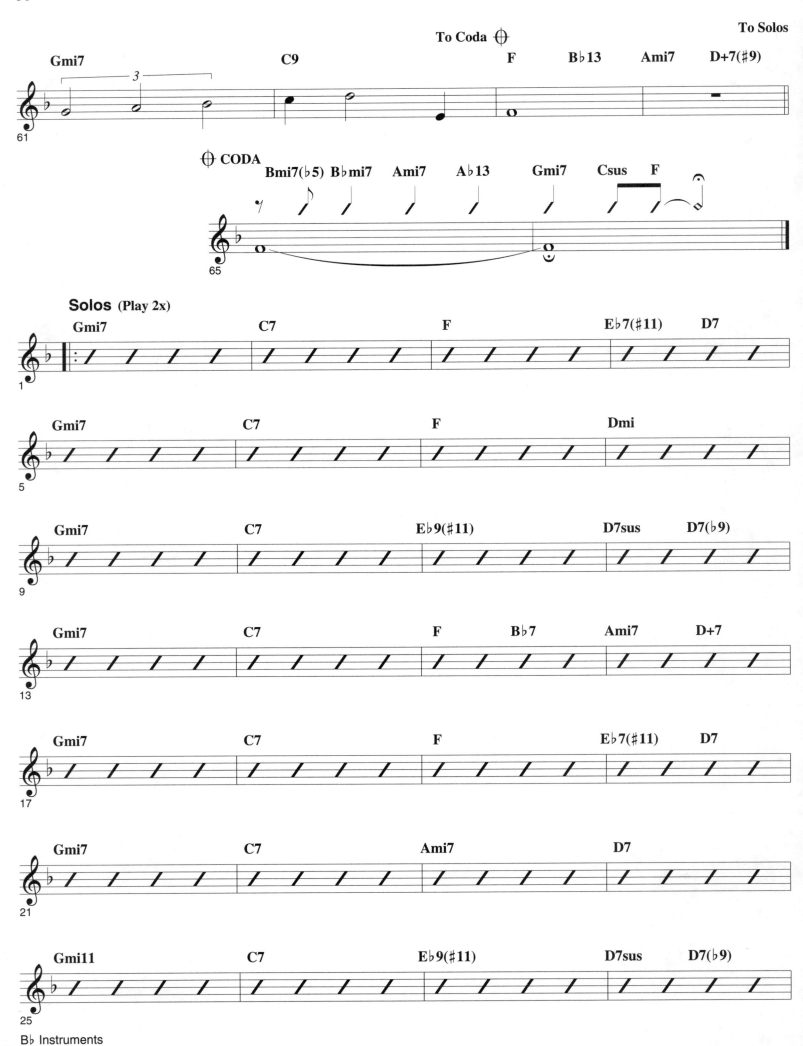

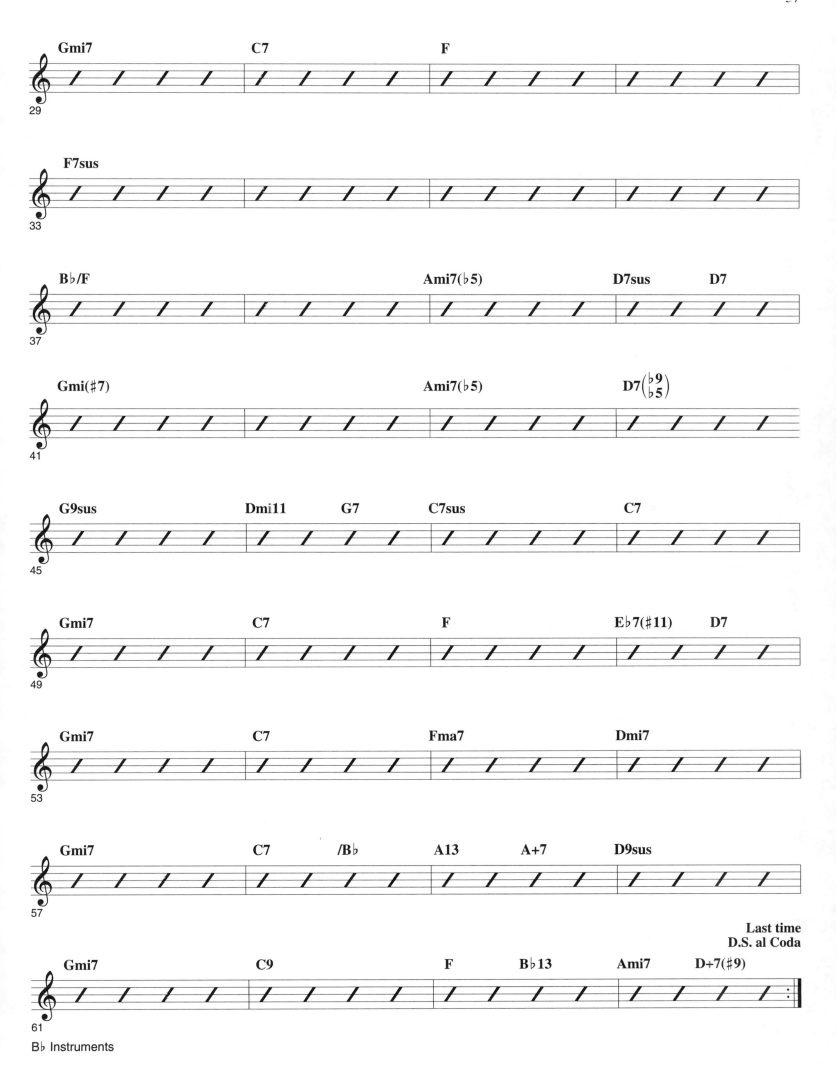

Last time
D.S. al Coda

Bb Instruments

EASY TO LOVE 13
(You'd Be So Easy to Love)
from BORN TO DANCE

Words and Music by
COLE PORTER

Bb Instruments

⊕ CODA

Solos (Play 5x)

Last time
D.S. al Coda

Bb Instruments

LET'S DO IT

(Let's Fall in Love)

Words and Music by
COLE PORTER

Bb Instruments

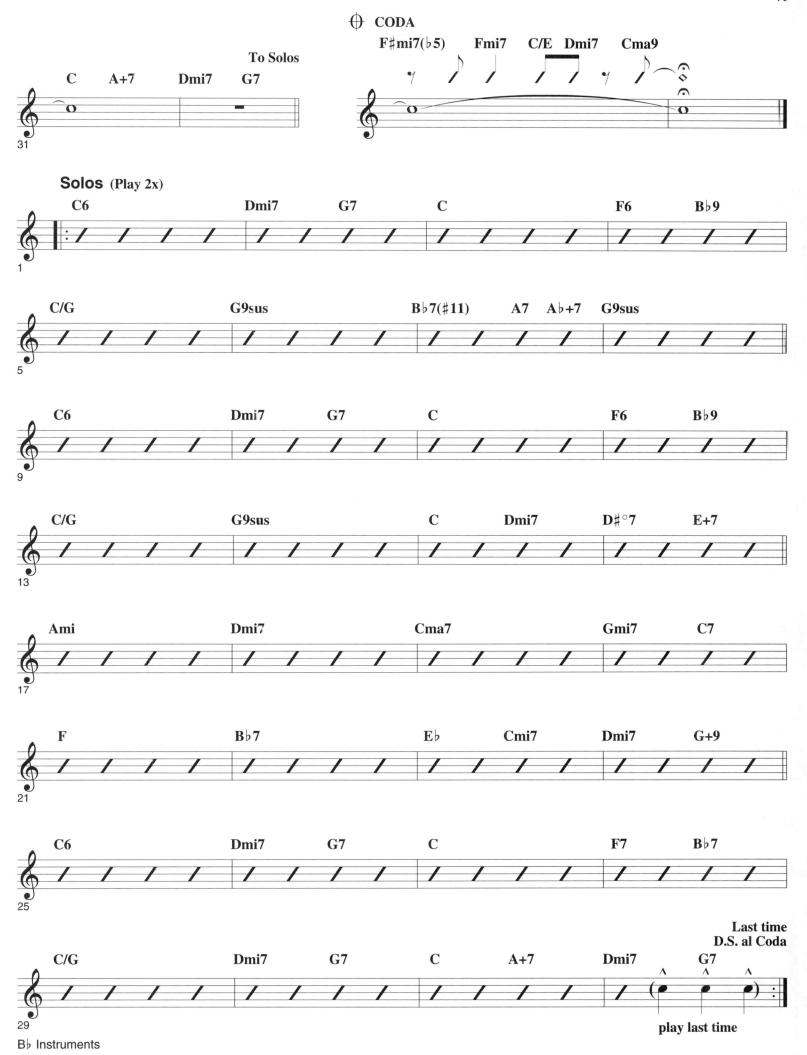

I'VE GOT YOU UNDER MY SKIN 15

from BORN TO DANCE

Words and Music by
COLE PORTER

Bb Instruments

Bb Instruments

44

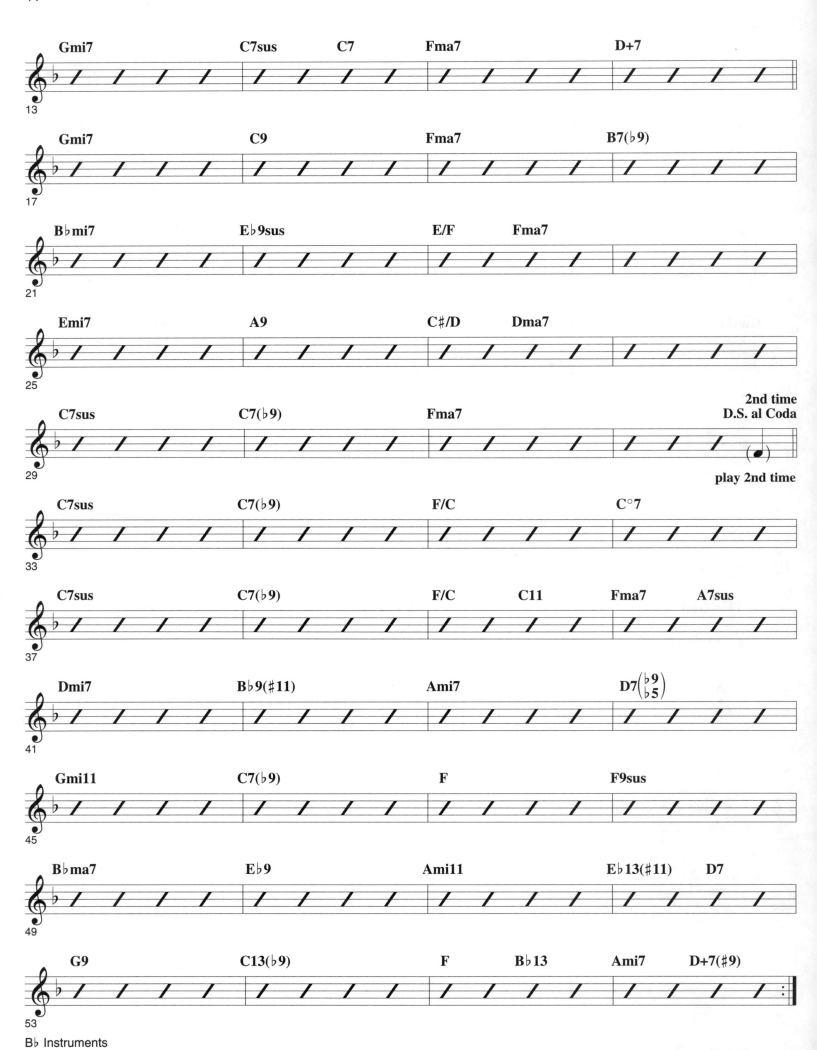

NIGHT AND DAY ◆16◆
from THE GAY DIVORCE

Words and Music by
COLE PORTER

Bb Instruments

B♭ Instruments

Bb Instruments

Jazz IMPROVISATION WORKSHOP

An exciting new improvisation method designed for all levels of players – from the absolute beginner to the experienced performer. Instructional volumes can be used individually or in a group/classroom environment. Play-along song collections feature musical variety, top-notch rhythm section accompaniment, great tunes, and performance of each head as well as choruses for improvisation. Each book includes a play-along CD.

PATTERNS FOR BEGINNING IMPROVISATION

For All Instruments • by Frank Mantooth

FROM THE BEGINNING

This beginning improvisation method is designed for students who are beginners in jazz – no prior jazz experience is necessary to use this book. The patterns begin simply and gradually increase in difficulty.

00841100 C Inst $17.95
00841101 Bb Inst............$17.95
00841102 Eb Inst............$17.95
00841103 Bass Clef $17.95

MOVIN' ON TO THE BLUES

This method for blues improvisation is designed for students with minimal jazz experience. Simple patterns are presented with easy, but frequently encountered progressions.

00841104 C Inst $17.95
00841105 Bb Inst............$17.95
00841106 Eb Inst............$17.95
00841107 Bass Clef $17.95

JAZZ STANDARDS PLAY-ALONG COLLECTIONS

JAZZ CLASSIC STANDARDS

15 songs, including: All Of Me • Don't Get Around Much Anymore • Milestones • My Funny Valentine • Opus One • When I Fall In Love • and more.

00841120 C Inst $17.95
00841121 Bb Inst......................$17.95
00841122 Eb Inst......................$17.95
00841123 Bass Clef $17.95

JAZZ FAVORITES

15 songs, including: Bewitched • Bye Bye Blackbird • How High The Moon • Now's The Time • Speak Low • and more.

00841124 C Inst $14.95
00841125 Bb Inst......................$14.95
00841126 Eb Inst......................$14.95
00841127 Bass Clef $14.95

ESSENTIAL JAZZ STANDARDS

15 songs, including: The Girl From Ipanema • Groovin' High • Have You Met Miss Jones? • It Could Happen To You • It Might As Well Be Spring • Long Ago And Far Away • A Night In Tunisia • Stella By Starlight • and more.

00841128 C Inst $14.95
00841129 Bb Inst......................$14.95
00841130 Eb Inst......................$14.95
00841131 Bass Clef $14.95

JAZZ GEMS

15 songs, including: All The Things You Are • Bluesette • Epistrophy • How Insensitive • My Funny Valentine • My Romance • Satin Doll • Summer Samba (So Nice) • Tangerine • and more.

00841132 C Inst $14.95
00841133 Bb Inst......................$14.95
00841134 Eb Inst......................$14.95
00841135 Bass Clef $14.95

FOR MORE INFORMATION, SEE YOUR LOCAL MUSIC DEALER,
OR WRITE TO:

HAL•LEONARD® CORPORATION

7777 W. BLUEMOUND RD. P.O. BOX 13819 MILWAUKEE, WI 53213

Visit Hal Leonard on the internet at http://www.halleonard.com

Prices, contents, and availability subject to change without notice. Some products may not be available outside the U.S.A.